21st Century
Basic Skills
Library

KIDS CAN MAKE MANNERS COUNT
SPEAK UP!

by Katie Marsico

3

Cherry Lake Publishing • Ann Arbor, Michigan

Published in the United States of America
by Cherry Lake Publishing
Ann Arbor, Michigan
www.cherrylakepublishing.com

Content Adviser: Tonia Bock, PhD, Associate Professor of Psychology,
St. Thomas University, St. Paul, Minnesota

Photo Credits: Cover and pages 1, 4, 6, 8, 10, 12, 16, 18, and 20,
©Denise Mondloch; page 14, ©Igor Bulgarin/Shutterstock, Inc.

Library of Congress Cataloging-in-Publication Data
Marsico, Katie, 1980–
  Speak up! / by Katie Marsico.
    p. cm.—(21st century basic skills library) (Kids can make manners
count)
  Includes bibliographical references and index.
  ISBN 978-1-61080-434-9 (lib. bdg.) — ISBN 978-1-61080-521-6 (e-book) —
ISBN 978-1-61080-608-4 (pbk.)
1. Oral communication—Juvenile literature. I. Title.
  P95.M334 2013
  395.1'22—dc23   2012001704

Cherry Lake Publishing would like to acknowledge
the work of The Partnership for 21st Century Skills.
Please visit *www.21stcenturyskills.org* for more information.

Printed in the United States of America
Corporate Graphics Inc.
July 2012
CLFA11

TABLE OF CONTENTS

A Matter of Mumbling

Alex had a great story to share in class.

His teacher Mrs. Neal called on him to speak.

The other students prepared to listen.

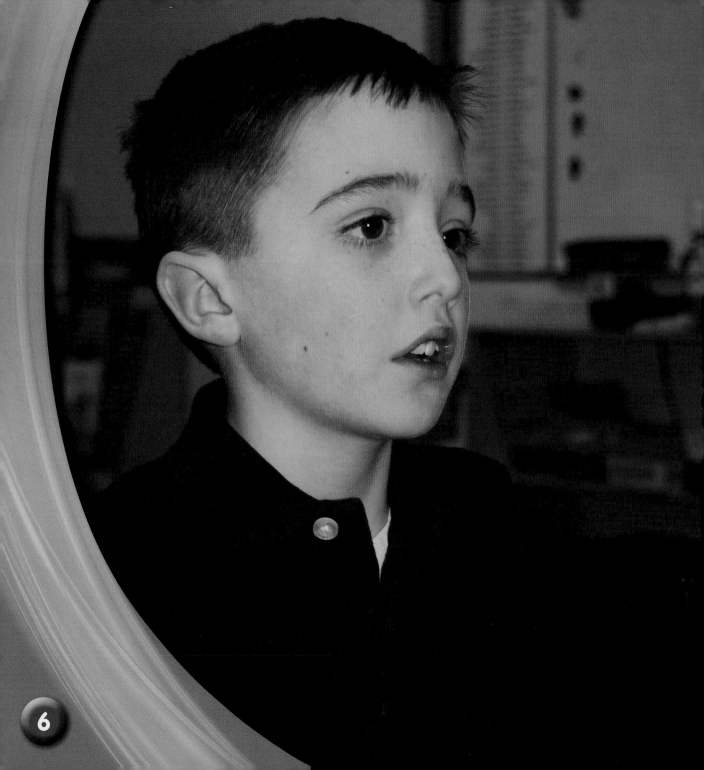

Alex became nervous.

He **mumbled** when he talked.

No one was able to hear him.
Everyone was **confused** by
Alex's story.

Making Manners Work

Alex wanted to share his story.

Yet he was often too quiet when he spoke.

Mrs. Neal had a **solution** to this problem.

Mrs. Neal told Alex that it was good **manners** to speak up.

Otherwise, people would not understand him.

Then they might feel confused.

Learning to Be Louder

Mrs. Neal told Alex to try taking a deep breath. She also said he should sit up straight.

This helps many speakers feel more **confident**.

Mrs. Neal said Alex should try out for the school play.

He spoke up when he acted onstage.

He wanted to be sure the **audience** heard his voice.

Mrs. Neal said Alex should speak up in class, too.

He liked telling stories. He took a deep breath when it was time to share.

18

Alex started speaking louder and clearer.

He was also careful not to talk too fast.

Alex watched people's faces to see if they understood him.

Soon everyone was enjoying Alex's stories.

His class heard him better because he spoke up.

Good manners made it easier for Alex to share!

Find Out More

BOOK

Burstein, John. *Speak Up! Communicating Confidently.*
 New York: Crabtree Publishing Company, 2011.

WEB SITE

U.S. Department of Health and Human Services—
Building Blocks: Manners Quiz
www.bblocks.samhsa.gov/family/activities/quizzes/manners.aspx
Take a fun online quiz to test how much you know about manners!

Glossary

audience (AW-dee-unts) people who gather to watch or listen to a performance

confident (KAN-fuh-dunt) sure of oneself

confused (kun-FYOOZD) not able to understand

manners (MA-nurz) behavior that is kind and polite

mumbled (MUM-buld) said something too quietly or not clearly enough for others to hear

solution (suh-LOO-shuhn) an answer to a problem

Home and School Connection

Use this list of words from the book to help your child become a better reader. Word games and writing activities can help beginning readers reinforce literacy skills.

a	deep	learning	on	soon	this
able	easier	liked	one	speak	time
acted	enjoying	listen	onstage	speaking	to
Alex	everyone	louder	other	speakers	told
Alex's	faces	made	otherwise	spoke	too
also	fast	making	out	started	took
and	feel	manners	people	stories	try
audience	for	many	people's	story	understand
be	good	matter	play	straight	understood
became	great	might	prepared	students	up
because	had	more	problem	sure	voice
better	he	Mrs.	quiet	taking	wanted
breath	hear	mumbled	said	talk	was
by	heard	mumbling	school	talked	watched
called	helps	Neal	see	teacher	when
careful	him	nervous	share	telling	work
class	his	no	she	that	would
clearer	if	not	should	the	yet
confident	in	of	sit	they	
confused	it	often	solution	then	

Index

About the Author

Katie Marsico is an author of children's and young-adult reference books. She lives outside of Chicago, Illinois, with her husband and children.